365 Days
to
Know Your
BIBLE

365 Days
to
Know Your
BIBLE

PAUL KENT

BARBOUR BOOKS
An Imprint of Barbour Publishing, Inc.

© 2014 by Barbour Publishing, Inc.

ISBN 978-1-64352-493-1

All rights reserved. No part of this publication may be reproduced or transmitted for commercial purposes, except for brief quotations in printed reviews, without written permission of the publisher.

Churches and other noncommercial interests may reproduce portions of this book without the express written permission of Barbour Publishing, provided that the text does not exceed 5 percent of the entire book and that the text is not material quoted from another publisher. When reproducing text from this book, include the following credit line: "From *365 Days to Know Your Bible*, published by Barbour Publishing, Inc. Used by permission."

Unless otherwise noted, all scripture is taken from the King James Version of the Bible.

Scripture quotations marked NIV are taken from the HOLY BIBLE, NEW INTERNATIONAL VERSION®. NIV®. Copyright © 1973, 1978, 1984, 2011 by Biblica, Inc.™ Used by permission. All rights reserved worldwide.

Published by Barbour Books, an imprint of Barbour Publishing, Inc., 1810 Barbour Drive, Uhrichsville, Ohio 44683, www.barbourbooks.com

Our mission is to inspire the world with the life-changing message of the Bible.

Printed in the United States of America.

INTRODUCTION

Through sixty-six separate books, 1,189 chapters, and hundreds of thousands of words, the Bible shares one extraordinary message: God loves you.

From the first chapter of Genesis, where God creates human beings, through the last chapter of Revelation, where God welcomes anyone to "take the water of life freely" (22:17), the Bible proves God is intimately involved in, familiar with, and concerned about the lives of people. His amazing love is shown in the death of His Son, Jesus Christ, on the cross. That sacrifice for sin allows anyone to be right with God through simple faith in Jesus' work.

These truths are found in the pages of scripture. But sometimes they can be obscured by the vast amount of information the Bible contains. That's why *365 Days to Know Your Bible* was written.

In this little book, you'll find brief surveys of all sixty-six Bible books, broken down into 365 short, daily readings. Each summarizes what that book is about—always within the context of God's love and concern for people. Every entry follows this outline:

- AUTHOR: who wrote the book, according to the Bible itself or ancient tradition

- DATE: when the book was written or the time the book covers

- IN TEN WORDS OR LESS: a "nutshell" glance at the book's key theme

- DETAILS, PLEASE: a synopsis of the key people, events, and messages covered in the book

- QUOTABLE: one, two, or several key verses from the book

- UNIQUE AND UNUSUAL: facts—some serious, some less so—that make the book stand out

Your Bible is certainly worth knowing. Use this book to begin a journey of discovery that could truly change your life!

Day 1

GENESIS

Author/Date

Not stated but traditionally attributed to Moses. Moses lived around the 1400s BC, but the events of Genesis date to the very beginning of time.

In Ten Words or Less

God creates the world and chooses a special people.

Day 2

Details, Please (part 1)

The Bible's first book never explains God; it simply assumes His existence: "In the beginning God. . ." (1:1). Chapters 1 and 2 describe how God created the universe and everything in it simply by speaking: "God said. . .and it was so" (1:6–7, 9, 11, 14–15). Humans, however, received special handling, as "God formed man of the dust of the ground, and breathed into his nostrils the breath of life" (2:7), and woman was crafted from a rib of man.

Day 3

DETAILS, PLEASE (PART 2)

The first two people, Adam and Eve, lived in perfection but ruined paradise by disobeying God at the urging of a "subtil" (crafty, 3:1) serpent. Sin throws humans into a moral freefall as the world's first child—Cain—murders his brother, Abel. People become so bad that God decides to flood the entire planet, saving only the righteous Noah, his family, and an ark (boat) full of animals.

Day 4

DETAILS, PLEASE (PART 3)

After the flood and repopulation of earth, God chooses a man named Abram as patriarch of a specially blessed people, later called "Israel" after an alternative name of Abram's grandson Jacob. Genesis ends with Jacob's son Joseph, by a miraculous chain of events, ruling in Egypt—setting up the events of the following book of Exodus.

Day 5

Quotable

- God said, Let there be light: and there was light. (1:3)
- Noah found grace in the eyes of the LORD. (6:8)
- He [Abram] believed in the LORD; and he counted it to him for righteousness. (15:6)

Day 6

Unique and Unusual

Genesis quickly introduces the concept of one God in multiple persons, a concept later called the Trinity: "God said, Let *us* make man in *our* image, after *our* likeness" (1:26, emphasis added). Also early on, God gives a hint of Jesus' future suffering and victory when He curses the serpent for deceiving Eve: "I will put enmity between thee and the woman, and between thy seed and her seed; it shall bruise thy head, and thou shalt bruise his heel" (3:15).

Day 7

EXODUS

Author/Date

Not stated but traditionally attributed to Moses. In Exodus 34:27 God tells Moses, "Write thou these words," and Jesus, in Mark 12:26, quotes from Exodus as "the book of Moses." Approximately the mid-1400s BC.

In Ten Words or Less

God delivers His people, the Israelites, from slavery in Egypt.

Day 8

Details, Please (Part 1)

The Israelites prosper in Egypt, having settled there at the invitation of Abraham's great-grandson Joseph, who entered the country as a slave and rose to second in command. When Joseph dies, a new pharaoh sees the burgeoning family as a threat—and makes the people his slaves.

Day 9

Details, Please (Part 2)

God hears the Israelites' groaning as slaves, remembering "his covenant with Abraham, with Isaac, and with Jacob" (2:24) and raising up Moses as their deliverer. God speaks through a burning bush, and Moses reluctantly agrees to demand the Israelites' release from Pharaoh.

Day 10

Details, Please (Part 3)

To break Pharaoh's will, God sends ten plagues on Egypt, ending with the death of every firstborn child—except those of the Israelites. They put sacrificial blood on their doorposts, causing the Lord to "pass over" (12:13) their homes. Pharaoh finally allows the Israelites to leave the country (the "Exodus"), and God parts the Red Sea for the people, who are being pursued by Egyptian soldiers.

Day 11

Details, Please (Part 4)

At Mount Sinai, God delivers the Ten Commandments, rules for worship, and laws to change the family into a nation. When Moses delays on the mountain, the people begin worshipping a golden calf, bringing a plague upon themselves. Moses returns to restore order, and Exodus ends with the people continuing their journey to the "promised land" of Canaan, following God's "pillar of cloud" by day and "pillar of fire" by night.

Day 12

Quotable

- God said unto Moses, I AM THAT I AM: and he said, Thus shalt thou say unto the children of Israel, I AM hath sent me unto you. (3:14)
- Thus saith the LORD, Let my people go. (8:1)
- Thou shalt have no other gods before me. (20:3)

Day 13

UNIQUE AND UNUSUAL

God told the Israelites to celebrate the "Passover" with a special meal of bread made without yeast (12:14–15). Three thousand years later, Jewish people still commemorate the event.

Day 14

LEVITICUS

AUTHOR/DATE

Not stated but traditionally attributed to Moses. Approximately the mid-1400s BC.

IN TEN WORDS OR LESS

A holy God explains how to worship Him.

Day 15

DETAILS, PLEASE (PART 1)

Leviticus, meaning "about the Levites," describes how that family line should lead the Israelites in worship. The book provides ceremonial laws as opposed to the moral laws of Exodus, describing offerings to God, dietary restrictions, and purification rites.

Day 16

DETAILS, PLEASE (PART 2)

In Leviticus special holy days—including the Sabbath, Passover, and Day of Atonement (Yom Kippur)—are commanded. The family of Aaron, Moses' brother, is ordained as Israel's formal priesthood. Leviticus lists several blessings for obedience and many more punishments for disobedience.

Day 17

Quotable

- Ye shall be holy; for I [God] am holy. (11:44)
- The life of the flesh is in the blood. . .it is the blood that maketh an atonement for the soul. (17:11)

Day 18

Unique and Unusual

Leviticus's blood sacrifices are contrasted with Jesus' death on the cross by the writer of Hebrews: "Who needeth not daily, as those high priests, to offer up sacrifice. . .for this he did once, when he offered up himself" (7:27).

Day 19

NUMBERS

Author/Date

Not stated but traditionally attributed to Moses. Approximately 1400 BC.

In Ten Words or Less

Faithless Israelites wander forty years in the wilderness of Sinai.

---*---

Day 20

Details, Please (Part 1)

Numbers begins with a census—hence the book's name. Fourteen months after the Israelites escape Egypt, they number 603,550 men, not including the Levites. This mass of people, the newly formed nation of Israel, begins a march of approximately two hundred miles to the "promised land" of Canaan—a journey that will take decades to complete.

Day 21

Details, Please (Part 2)

The delay in entering Canaan is God's punishment of the people, who complain about food and water, rebel against Moses, and hesitate to enter Canaan because of powerful people already living there. God decrees that this entire generation will die in the wilderness, leaving the Promised Land to a new generation of more obedient Israelites.

Day 22

Quotable

- The LORD is longsuffering, and of great mercy, forgiving iniquity and transgression. (14:18)

Day 23

Unique and Unusual

Even Moses misses out on the Promised Land,
punishment for disobeying God by striking, rather
than speaking to, a rock from which water would
miraculously appear (20:1–13).

Day 24

DEUTERONOMY

Authors/Date

Traditionally attributed to Moses, an idea supported
by Deuteronomy 31:9: "Moses wrote this law,
and delivered it unto the priests. . .and unto all the
elders of Israel." Chapter 34, recording Moses'
death, was probably written by his successor,
Joshua. Approximately 1400 BC.

In Ten Words or Less

Moses reminds the Israelites of their history and
God's laws.

Day 25

Details, Please (Part 1)

With a name meaning "second law," Deuteronomy records Moses' final words as the Israelites prepare to enter the Promised Land. Forty years have passed since God handed down His laws on Mount Sinai, and the entire generation that experienced that momentous event has died. So Moses reminds the new generation both of God's commands and of their national history as they ready their entry into Canaan.

Day 26

Details, Please (Part 2)

The invasion of Canaan will occur under Joshua, as Moses will only *see* the Promised Land from Mount Nebo. "So Moses the servant of the Lord died there. . . . And he [God] buried him in a valley in the land of Moab. . .but no man knoweth of his sepulchre unto this day" (34:5–6). Moses was 120 years old.

Day 27

QUOTABLE

- Hear, O Israel: The LORD our God is one LORD. (6:4)
- Thou shalt love the LORD thy God with all thine heart, and with all thy soul, and with all thy might. (6:5)
- The LORD thy God is a jealous God among you. (6:15)

Day 28

UNIQUE AND UNUSUAL

The New Testament quotes from Deuteronomy dozens of times, including three from the story of Jesus' temptation in the wilderness in Matthew 4:1–11. The Lord defeated Satan by restating Deuteronomy 8:3 ("Man shall not live by bread alone, but by every word that proceedeth out of the mouth of God"); 6:16 ("Thou shalt not tempt the Lord thy God"); and 6:13 ("Thou shalt worship the Lord thy God, and him only shalt thou serve").

The Ten Commandments, also found in Exodus 20, are restated in Deuteronomy 5.

Day 29

JOSHUA

Author/Date

Traditionally attributed to Joshua himself, except for the final five verses (24:29–33), which describe Joshua's death and legacy. Approximately 1375 BC.

In Ten Words or Less

The Israelites capture and settle the promised land of Canaan.

Day 30

Details, Please (Part 1)

With Moses and an entire generation of disobedient Israelites dead, God tells Joshua to lead the people into Canaan, their promised land. In Jericho, the city that is their first major obstacle, the prostitute Rahab helps Israelite spies and earns protection from the destruction of the city: God knocks its walls flat as Joshua's army marches outside, blowing trumpets and shouting.

Day 31

Details, Please (Part 2)

Joshua leads a successful military campaign to clear idol-worshipping people—Hittites, Amorites, Canaanites, Perizzites, Hivites, and Jebusites— from the land. At one point, God answers Joshua's prayer to make the sun stand still, allowing more time to complete a battle (10:1–15).

Day 32

Details, Please (Part 3)

With major cities subdued, Joshua divides the land among the twelve tribes of Israel, reminding the people to stay true to the God who led them home: "Now therefore put away. . .the strange gods which are among you, and incline your heart unto the Lord God of Israel" (24:23).

Day 33

Quotable

- Be strong and of a good courage; be not afraid, neither be thou dismayed: for the LORD thy God is with thee whithersoever thou goest. (1:9)
- One man of you shall chase a thousand: for the LORD your God, he it is that fighteth for you, as he hath promised you. (23:10)
- Choose you this day whom ye will serve. . .as for me and my house, we will serve the LORD. (24:15)

Day 34

Unique and Unusual (Part 1)

Joshua is one of few major Bible characters who seemed to do everything right—he was a strong leader, completely committed to God, who never fell into recorded sin or disobedience. Only one mistake mars his record: Joshua's experience with the Gibeonites, one of the local groups he should have destroyed, but failed to do so.

Day 35

UNIQUE AND UNUSUAL (PART 2)

The Gibeonites, fearing for their lives, appeared
before Joshua dressed in old clothes, carrying
dry, moldy bread, claiming they had come from
a faraway land. Joshua and the Israelite leaders
"asked not counsel at the mouth of the LORD"
(9:14) and agreed to a peace treaty. When Joshua
learned the truth, he honored his agreement with
the Gibeonites—but made them slaves.

Day 36

JUDGES

AUTHOR/DATE

Unknown; some suggest the prophet Samuel.
Written approximately 1050 BC, covering
events that occurred as far back as 1375 BC.

IN TEN WORDS OR LESS

Israel goes through cycles of sin, suffering,
and salvation.

Day 37

Details, Please (Part 1)

After Joshua's death, the Israelites lose momentum in driving pagan people out of the Promised Land. "The children of Benjamin did not drive out the Jebusites that inhabited Jerusalem" (1:21) is a statement characteristic of many tribes, which allow idol worshippers to stay in their midst—with tragic results.

Day 38

Details, Please (Part 2)

"Ye have not obeyed my voice" God says to His people. "They shall be as thorns in your sides, and their gods shall be a snare unto you" (2:2–3). That's exactly what happens, as the Israelites begin a cycle of worshipping idols, suffering punishment by attackers.

Day 39

Details, Please (Part 3)

The Israelites respond to the attackers by crying to God for help, and receiving God's aid in the form of a human judge (or "deliverer") who restores order. Lesser-known judges include Othniel, Ehud, Tola, Jair, and Jephthah, while more familiar figures include Deborah, the only female judge, who led a military victory against the Canaanites.

Day 40

Details, Please (Part 4)

Another judge, Gideon, tested God's will with a fleece and defeated the armies of Midian. Samson, the amazingly strong judge, defeated the Philistines. Samson's great weakness—his love for unsavory women such as Delilah—led to his downfall and death in a Philistine temple.

Day 41

Quotable

- They forsook the LORD God of their fathers, which brought them out of the land of Egypt, and followed other gods, of the gods of the people that were round about them. (2:12)
- The LORD raised up judges, which delivered them out of the hand of those that spoiled them. (2:16)
- The LORD said unto Gideon, The people that are with thee are too many for me to give the Midianites into their hands, lest Israel vaunt themselves against me, saying, Mine own hand hath saved me. (7:2)

Day 42

Unique and Unusual

Several judges had unusual families by today's standards: Jair had thirty sons (10:4), Abdon had forty sons (12:14), and Ibzan had thirty sons and thirty daughters (12:9). Jephthah had only one child, a daughter, whom he foolishly vowed to sacrifice to God in exchange for a military victory (11:30–40).

Day 43

RUTH

Author/Date

Not stated; some suggest Samuel. Ruth, the great-grandmother of King David (who reigned approximately 1010–970 BC), probably lived around 1100 BC.

In Ten Words or Less

Loyal daughter-in-law pictures God's faithfulness, love, and care.

Day 44

Details, Please (Part 1)

Ruth, a Gentile woman, marries into a Jewish family. When all of the men of the family die, Ruth shows loyalty to her mother-in-law, Naomi, staying with her and scavenging food to keep them alive.

Day 45

DETAILS, PLEASE (PART 2)

As Ruth gleans barley in a field of the wealthy
Boaz, he takes an interest in her and orders his
workers to watch over her and leave extra grain for
her to glean. Naomi recognizes Boaz as her late
husband's relative.

Day 46

DETAILS, PLEASE (PART 3)

Naomi encourages Ruth to pursue Boaz as a "kins-
man redeemer," one who weds a relative's widow
to continue a family line. Boaz marries Ruth, has a
son, Obed, starting a prominent family.

Day 47

Quotable

- Whither thou goest, I will go; and where thou lodgest, I will lodge: thy people shall be my people, and thy God my God. (1:16)

Day 48

Unique and Unusual

Ruth, from the pagan land of Moab, married a Jewish man and became the great-grandmother of Israel's greatest king, David—and an ancestor of Jesus Christ.

Day 49

1 SAMUEL

AUTHOR/DATE

Not stated. Samuel himself was likely involved, though some of the history of 1 Samuel occurs after the prophet's death. Approximately 1100–1000 BC.

IN TEN WORDS OR LESS

Israel's twelve tribes unite under a king.

Day 50

DETAILS, PLEASE (PART 1)

An infertile woman, Hannah, begs God for a son, promising to return him to the Lord's service. Samuel is born and soon sent to the temple to serve under the aging priest, Eli. Upon Eli's death, Samuel serves as judge, or deliverer, of Israel.

Day 51

Details, Please (Part 2)

Samuel subdues the nation's fearsome enemy, the Philistines. As Samuel ages, Israel's tribal leaders reject his sinful sons and ask for a king. Samuel warns that a king will tax the people and force them into service, but they insist. God tells Samuel to anoint the notably tall and handsome Saul as Israel's first ruler.

Day 52

Details, Please (Part 3)

King Saul starts well but begins making poor choices—and when he offers a sacrifice to God, a job reserved for priests, Samuel tells Saul that he will be replaced. Saul's successor will be a shepherd named David, who with God's help kills a giant Philistine warrior named Goliath. David becomes Israel's hero.

Day 53

Details, Please (Part 4)

The jealous king seeks to kill David, who runs for his life. David rejects opportunities to kill Saul himself, saying, "I would not stretch forth mine hand against the LORD's anointed" (26:23). At the end of 1 Samuel, Saul dies battling the Philistines, making way for David to become king.

※

Day 54

Quotable

- The LORD said unto Samuel. . .they have not rejected thee, but they have rejected me, that I should not reign over them. (8:7)
- Behold, to obey is better than sacrifice, and to hearken than the fat of rams. (15:22)
- Then said David to the Philistine [Goliath], Thou comest to me with a sword, and with a spear, and with a shield: but I come to thee in the name of the LORD of hosts, the God of the armies of Israel, whom thou hast defied. (17:45)

Day 55

Unique and Unusual

The future King Saul is a donkey herder (9:5) who tries to hide from his own coronation (10:21–22). As king, Saul breaks his own law by asking a medium to call up the spirit of the dead Samuel (chapter 28).

Day 56

2 SAMUEL

Author/Date

Unknown but not Samuel—since the events of the book take place after his death. Some suggest Abiathar the priest (15:35). Approximately 1010–970 BC, the reign of King David.

In Ten Words or Less

David becomes Israel's greatest king—but with major flaws.

Day 57

Details, Please (Part 1)

When King Saul dies, David is made king by the southern Jewish tribe of Judah. Seven years later, after the death of Saul's son Ish-bosheth, king of the northern tribes, David becomes ruler of all Israel.

---※---

Day 58

Details, Please (Part 2)

After capturing Jerusalem from the Jebusites, David creates a new capital for his unified nation, and God promises David, "Your throne will be established forever" (7:16 NIV). Military victories make Israel strong, but when David stays home from battle one spring, he commits adultery with a beautiful neighbor, Bathsheba. Then he has her husband—one of his soldiers—murdered.

Day 59

Details, Please (Part 3)

Following the murder of Bathsheba's husband, the prophet Nathan confronts David with a story of a rich man who steals a poor man's sheep. David is furious until Nathan announces, "Thou art the man" (12:7). Chastened, David repents and God forgives his sins—but their consequences will affect David powerfully. The baby conceived in the tryst dies, and David's family begins to splinter apart.

Day 60

Details, Please (Part 4)

As David's family splinters, one of David's sons, Amnon, rapes his half sister, and a second son, Absalom—full brother to the violated girl—kills Amnon in revenge. Absalom then conspires to steal the kingdom from David, causing his father to flee for his life.

Day 61

Details, Please (Part 5)

Absalom's revolt ends when he dies in battle with David's men, David grieves so deeply that he offends his soldiers. Ultimately, David returns to Jerusalem to reassert his kingship. He also raises another son born to Bathsheba—Solomon.

Day 62

Quotable

- How are the mighty fallen in the midst of the battle! (1:25)
- Who am I, O Lord God? and what is my house, that thou hast brought me hitherto? (7:18)
- O my son Absalom, my son, my son Absalom! would God I had died for thee, O Absalom, my son, my son! (18:33)

Day 63

Unique and Unusual

David's nephew killed a Philistine "of great stature, that had on every hand six fingers, and on every foot six toes" (21:20). David's top soldier, Adino, once killed 800 men single-handedly (23:8).

Day 64

1 KINGS

Author/Date

Not stated and unknown; one early tradition claimed Jeremiah wrote 1 and 2 Kings. Covering events from about 970 to 850 BC, 1 Kings was probably written sometime after the Babylonian destruction of Jerusalem in 586 BC.

In Ten Words or Less

Israel divides into rival northern and southern nations.

Day 65

Details, Please (Part 1)

King David, in declining health, names Solomon, his son with Bathsheba, successor. After David's death, God speaks to Solomon in a dream, offering him anything he'd like—and Solomon chooses wisdom.

Day 66

Details, Please (Part 2)

God gives Solomon great wisdom, along with much power and wealth. The new king soon builds God a permanent temple in Jerusalem, and the Lord visits Solomon again to promise blessings for obedience and trouble for disobedience.

Day 67

Details, Please (Part 3)

Sadly, Solomon's wisdom fails him, as he marries
seven hundred women, many of them foreigners
who turn his heart to idols. When Solomon dies,
his son Rehoboam foolishly antagonizes the people
of Israel, and only the two southern tribes remain
under him. They continue under Solomon's line
in a nation called Judah.

Day 68

Details, Please (Part 4)

The ten northern tribes form their own nation
under Jeroboam, a former official of Solomon's.

Jeroboam begins badly, initiating idol worship
in the north; many wicked rulers follow. Judah,
the two southern tribes, will also have many poor
leaders, though occasional kings, such as Asa and
Jehoshaphat, follow the Lord.

Day 69

Details, Please (Part 5)

1 Kings introduces the prophet Elijah, who confronts the evil King Ahab and Queen Jezebel of Israel regarding their worship of the false god Baal. In God's power, Elijah defeats 450 false prophets in a dramatic contest on Mount Carmel.

Day 70

Quotable

- David drew nigh that he should die; and he charged Solomon his son, saying, I go the way of all the earth: be thou strong therefore, and shew thyself a man. (2:1–2)
- Give therefore thy servant an understanding heart to judge thy people, that I may discern between good and bad: for who is able to judge this thy so great a people? (3:9)
- Hear me, O LORD, hear me, that this people may know that thou art the LORD God, and that thou hast turned their heart back again. (18:37)

Day 71

Unique and Unusual

Scholars say 1 and 2 Kings were originally a single volume and were split in half to allow for copying onto normal-sized scrolls.

Day 72

2 KINGS

Author/Date

Not stated and unknown; one early tradition claimed Jeremiah wrote 1 and 2 Kings. Covering about three hundred years from the 800s BC on, 2 Kings was probably written sometime after the Babylonian destruction of Jerusalem in 586 BC.

In Ten Words or Less

Both Jewish nations are destroyed for their disobedience to God.

Day 73

Details, Please (Part 1)

In 2 Kings the story of the kings continues, with more bad rulers, a handful of good ones, some familiar prophets, and the ultimate loss of the two Jewish nations. Early in 2 Kings, Elijah becomes the second man (after Enoch in Genesis 5:24) to go straight to heaven without dying.

Day 74

Details, Please (Part 2)

Elijah's successor, Elisha, performs many miracles and shares God's word with the "average people" of Israel. The northern kingdom's rulers are entirely wicked, and Israel, under its last king, Hoshea, is "carried. . .away into Assyria" (17:6) in 722 BC.

Day 75

Details, Please (Part 3)

Judah, with occasional good kings such as Hezekiah and Josiah, lasts a few years longer—but in 586 BC the southern kingdom's capital of Jerusalem "was broken up" (25:4) by Babylonian armies under King Nebuchadnezzar. They took everything valuable from the temple and the Jewish king's palace.

Day 76

Details, Please (Part 4)

The Babylonians also "carried away all Jerusalem, and all the princes, and all the mighty men of valour, even ten thousand captives, and all the craftsmen and smiths" (24:14). Ending on a slight up note, 2 Kings describes a new king of Babylon, Evil-merodach, showing kindness to Jehoiachin, the last real king of Judah, by giving him a place of honor in the Babylonian court.

Day 77

Quotable

- Behold, there appeared a chariot of fire, and horses of fire, and parted them both asunder; and Elijah went up by a whirlwind into heaven. (2:11)
- The LORD rejected all the seed of Israel, and afflicted them, and delivered them into the hand of spoilers, until he had cast them out of his sight. (17:20)
- So Judah was carried away out of their land. (25:21)

Day 78

Unique and Unusual

Isaiah, who wrote a long prophecy that appears later in the Old Testament, is prominent in 2 Kings 19. One of Judah's best kings, Josiah, was only eight years old when he took the throne (22:1).

Day 79

1 CHRONICLES

Author/Date

Not stated but traditionally attributed to Ezra the priest. Covers the history of Israel from about 1010 BC (the death of King Saul) to about 970 BC (the death of King David).

In Ten Words or Less

King David's reign is detailed and analyzed.

---※---

Day 80

Details, Please (Part 1)

1 Chronicles provides a history of Israel, going as far back as Adam, listing descendants, pausing to elaborate on Jabez who was more honorable than his brethren. By the eleventh chapter, the story turns to Israel's greatest king, David.

Day 81

Details, Please (Part 2)

1 Chronicles gives special emphasis on David's leadership of national worship. Another important focus of 1 Chronicles is on God's promise that David would have an eternal kingly line through his descendant Jesus Christ.

---※---

Day 82

Quotable

- I will settle him in mine house and in my kingdom for ever: and his throne shall be established for evermore. (17:14)

Day 83

UNIQUE AND UNUSUAL

1 Chronicles covers much of the same information as 2 Samuel, but without some of the seedier aspects of David's life—such as his adultery with Bathsheba and the engineered killing of her husband, Uriah.

Day 84

2 CHRONICLES

AUTHOR/DATE

Not stated but traditionally attributed to Ezra the priest. Covers Israelite history from about 970 BC (the accession of King Solomon) to the 500s BC (when exiled Jews returned to Jerusalem).

IN TEN WORDS OR LESS

The history of Israel from Solomon to division to destruction.

Day 85

Details, Please (Part 1)

David's son Solomon is made king, builds the temple, and becomes one of the most prominent rulers ever. But when he dies, the Jewish nation divides into ten northern tribes and two southern tribes.

Day 86

Details, Please (Part 2)

In the remainder of 2 Chronicles, the various kings of the relatively godlier southern nation of Judah are profiled right down to the destruction of Jerusalem by the Babylonians. The book ends with the Persian king Cyrus allowing Jews to rebuild the devastated temple.

Day 87

Quotable

- LORD God of Israel, there is no God like thee in the heaven, nor in the earth; which keepest covenant, and shewest mercy unto thy servants, that walk before thee with all their hearts. (6:14)

Day 88

Unique and Unusual

Continuing the positive spin of 1 Chronicles (the two books were originally one), 2 Chronicles ends with two verses that exactly repeat the first three verses of Ezra.

Day 89

EZRA

Author/Date

Not stated but traditionally attributed to Ezra
the priest (7:11). Approximately 530 BC to
the mid-400s BC.

In Ten Words or Less

Spiritual renewal begins after the Jews return from
exile.

---※---

Day 90

Details, Please (Part 1)

About a half century after Babylonians sacked
Jerusalem and carried Jews into captivity, Persia is
the new world power. King Cyrus allows a group
of exiles to return to Judah to rebuild the temple.
Some 42,000 people return and resettle the land.

Day 91

Details, Please (Part 2)

About seventy years later, Ezra is part of a smaller group that also returns to Judah. He teaches the law to the people, who have fallen away from God to the point of intermarrying with nearby pagan nations, something that was strictly forbidden by Moses (Deuteronomy 7:1–3).

Day 92

Quotable

- Ezra had prepared his heart to seek the law of the LORD, and to do it, and to teach in Israel statutes and judgments. (7:10)

Day 93

Unique and Unusual

Though God has said that he hates divorce (see Malachi 2:16 NIV), Ezra urged Jewish men to separate from their foreign wives.

———— ✳ ————

Day 94

NEHEMIAH

Author/Date

"The words of Nehemiah" (1:1), though Jewish tradition says those words were put on paper by Ezra. Approximately 445 BC.

In Ten Words or Less

Returning Jewish exiles rebuild the broken walls of Jerusalem.

Day 95

Details, Please (Part 1)

Nehemiah serves as "the king's cupbearer" (1:11) in Shushan, Persia. As a Jew, he's disturbed to learn that even though exiles have been back in Judah for nearly a hundred years, they have not rebuilt the city's walls, devastated by the Babylonians in 586 BC.

Day 96

Details, Please (Part 2)

Nehemiah asks and receives the king's permission to return to Jerusalem, where he leads a team of builders—against much pagan opposition—in reconstructing the walls in only fifty-two days. The quick work on the project shocks the Jews' enemies, who "perceived that this work was wrought of our God" (6:16).

Day 97

Quotable

- Think upon me, my God, for good, according to all that I have done for this people. (5:19)

---※---

Day 98

Unique and Unusual

Indignant over some fellow Jews' intermarriage with pagans, Nehemiah "cursed them, and smote certain of them, and plucked off their hair" (13:25).

Day 99

ESTHER

Author/Date

Not stated but perhaps Ezra or Nehemiah.
Approximately 486–465 BC, during the
reign of King Ahasuerus of Persia. Esther
became queen around 479 BC.

In Ten Words or Less

Beautiful Jewish girl becomes queen, saves fellow
Jews from slaughter.

Day 100

Details, Please (Part 1)

In a nationwide beauty contest, young Esther
becomes queen of Persia without revealing her
Jewish heritage. When a royal official plots to
kill every Jew in the country, Esther risks her
own life to request the king's protection.

Day 101

Details, Please (Part 2)

The king, pleased with Esther, is shocked by his official's plan to kill the Jews and has the man hanged—while decreeing that the Jews should defend themselves against the planned slaughter. Esther's people prevail and commemorate the event with a holiday called Purim.

Day 102

Quotable

- Esther obtained favour in the sight of all them that looked upon her. (2:15)
- Who knoweth whether thou art come to the kingdom for such a time as this? (4:14)

Day 103

Unique and Unusual

God's name is never mentioned in the book of Esther. Neither is prayer, though Esther asks her fellow Jews to fast for her before she approaches the king (4:16).

Day 104

JOB

Author/Date

Not stated. Unclear, but many believe Job is one of the oldest stories in the Bible, perhaps from approximately 2000 BC.

In Ten Words or Less

God allows human suffering for His own purposes.

Day 105

Details, Please (Part 1)

Head of a large family, Job is a wealthy farmer from a place called Uz. He's "perfect and upright" (1:1)—so much so, that God calls Satan's attention to him. The devil, unimpressed, asks and receives God's permission to attack Job's possessions—and wipes out thousands of sheep, camels, oxen, donkeys, and worst of all, Job's ten children.

Day 106

Details, Please (Part 2)

Despite Satan's attack, Job keeps his faith. Satan then receives God's permission to attack Job's health—but in spite of terrible physical suffering, Job refuses to "curse God, and die" as his wife suggests (2:9). Before long, though, Job begins to question why God would allow him—a good man—to suffer so severely.

Day 107

Details, Please (Part 3)

Job's suffering is worsened by the arrival of four "friends" who begin to accuse him of causing his own trouble by secret sin. "Is not thy wickedness great?" asks Eliphaz the Temanite (22:5). In the end, God Himself speaks, vindicating Job before his friends and also addressing the overarching issue of human suffering.

Day 108

Details, Please (Part 4)

God doesn't explain Job's suffering but asks a series of questions that shows His vast knowledge— implying that Job should simply trust God's way. And Job does, telling God, "I know that thou canst do every thing" (42:2). By story's end, God has restored Job's health, possessions, and family, giving him ten more children.

Day 109

Quotable

- Naked came I out of my mother's womb, and naked shall I return thither: the LORD gave, and the LORD hath taken away; blessed be the name of the LORD. (1:21)
- Man that is born of a woman is of few days and full of trouble. (14:1)
- I abhor myself, and repent in dust and ashes. (42:6)

Day 110

Unique and Unusual

The book of Job pictures Satan coming into God's presence (1:6). It also gives a clear Old Testament hint of Jesus' work when Job says, "I know that my redeemer liveth, and that he shall stand at the latter day upon the earth" (19:25).

Day 111

PSALMS

Authors/Date

Various, with nearly half attributed to King David. Other names noted include Solomon, Moses, Asaph, Ethan, and the sons of Korah. Many psalms don't mention an author. Approximately the 1400s BC (Moses' time) through the 500s BC (the time of the Jews' Babylonian exile).

In Ten Words or Less

Ancient Jewish songbook showcases prayers, praise—and complaints—to God.

Day 112

Details, Please (Part 1)

Over several centuries, God led various individuals to compose emotionally charged poems—of which 150 were later compiled into the book we know as Psalms. Many of the psalms are described as "of David," meaning they could be *by*, *for*, or *about* Israel's great king.

Day 113

Details, Please (Part 2)

Highlights of the book include the "shepherd psalm" (23), which describes God as protector and provider; David's cry for forgiveness after his sin with Bathsheba (51); psalms of praise (100 is a powerful example); and the celebration of scripture found in Psalm 119, with almost all of the 176 verses making some reference to God's laws, statutes, commandments, precepts, word, and the like.

Day 114

Details, Please (Part 3)

Some psalms, called "imprecatory," call for God's judgment on enemies (see Psalms 69 and 109, for example). Many psalms express agony of spirit on the writer's part—but nearly every psalm returns to the theme of praise to God. That's the way the book of Psalms ends: "Let every thing that hath breath praise the LORD. Praise ye the LORD" (150:6).

Day 115

QUOTABLE (PART 1)

- LORD, our Lord, how excellent is thy name in all the earth! (8:1)
- The LORD is my shepherd; I shall not want. (23:1)
- Create in me a clean heart, O God; and renew a right spirit within me. (51:10)

Day 116

QUOTABLE (PART 2)

- Thy word have I hid in mine heart, that I might not sin against thee. (119:11)
- I will lift up mine eyes unto the hills, from whence cometh my help. My help cometh from the LORD. (121:1–2)
- Behold, how good and how pleasant it is for brethren to dwell together in unity! (133:1)

Day 117

Unique and Unusual

The book of Psalms is the Bible's longest in terms of both number of chapters (150) and total word count. It contains the longest chapter in the Bible (Psalm 119, with 176 verses) and the shortest (Psalm 117, with 2 verses). Psalm 117 is also the midpoint of the Protestant Bible, with 594 chapters before it and 594 after.

Day 118

PROVERBS

Authors/Date

Primarily Solomon (1:1), with sections attributed to "the wise" (22:17), Agur (30:1), and King Lemuel (31:1). Little is known of the latter two. Solomon reigned approximately 970–930 BC. The staff of King Hezekiah, who lived about two hundred years later, "copied out" the latter chapters of the book we have today (25:1).

In Ten Words or Less

Pithy, memorable sayings encourage people to pursue wisdom.

Day 119

Details, Please (Part 1)

Proverbs doesn't have a story line—it's simply a collection of practical tips for living. Mainly from the pen of King Solomon, the wisest human being ever (in 1 Kings 3:12 God said, "I have given thee a wise and an understanding heart; so that there was none like thee before thee, neither after thee shall any arise like unto thee").

Day 120

Details, Please (Part 2)

The proverbs speak to issues such as work, money, sex, temptation, drinking, laziness, discipline, and child rearing. Underlying each proverb is the truth that "the fear of the LORD is the beginning of knowledge" (1:7).

Day 121

Quotable (Part 1)

- Trust in the LORD with all thine heart; and lean not unto thine own understanding. (3:5)
- Go to the ant, thou sluggard; consider her ways, and be wise. (6:6)
- A wise son maketh a glad father: but a foolish son is the heaviness of his mother. (10:1)

Day 122

Quotable (Part 2)

- As a jewel of gold in a swine's snout, so is a fair woman which is without discretion. (11:22)
- He that spareth his rod hateth his son: but he that loveth him chasteneth him betimes. (13:24)
- A soft answer turneth away wrath: but grievous words stir up anger. (15:1)

Day 123

Quotable (Part 3)

- Commit thy works unto the LORD, and thy thoughts shall be established. (16:3)
- Even a fool, when he holdeth his peace, is counted wise. (17:28)
- The name of the LORD is a strong tower: the righteous runneth into it, and is safe. (18:10)

Day 124

Quotable (Part 4)

- A good name is rather to be chosen than great riches. (22:1)
- Answer not a fool according to his folly, lest thou also be like unto him. (26:4)
- Faithful are the wounds of a friend. (27:6)

Day 125

Unique and Unusual

The final chapter of Proverbs includes a long poem in praise of wives, rather unusual for that time and culture.

Day 126

ECCLESIASTES

Author/Date

Not stated but probably Solomon. The author is identified as "the son of David" (1:1) and "king over Israel in Jerusalem" (1:12) and says he had "more wisdom than all they that have been before me" (1:16). Approximately 900s BC.

In Ten Words or Less

Apart from God, life is empty and unsatisfying.

Day 127

Details, Please (Part 1)

A king pursues the things of this world, only to find them unfulfilling. Learning, pleasure, work, laughter —"all is vanity" (1:2). The king also laments the inequities of life: People live, work hard, and die, only to leave their belongings to someone else.

Day 128

Details, Please (Part 2)

The king laments that the wicked prosper over the righteous; the poor are oppressed. Nevertheless, the king realizes "the conclusion of the whole matter: Fear God, and keep his commandments: for this is the whole duty of man" (12:13).

Day 129

QUOTABLE

- To every thing there is a season, and a time to every purpose under the heaven. (3:1)
- Remember now thy Creator in the days of thy youth. (12:1)

Day 130

UNIQUE AND UNUSUAL

The book's generally negative tone makes some readers wonder if Solomon wrote it late in life, after his hundreds of wives led him to stray from God.

Day 131

SONG OF SOLOMON

Author/Date

Solomon (1:1), though some wonder if the song "of Solomon" is like the psalms "of David"—which could mean they are *by*, *for*, or *about* him. Solomon ruled around 970–930 BC.

In Ten Words or Less

Married love is a beautiful thing worth celebrating.

Day 132

Details, Please

A dark-skinned beauty is marrying the king, and both are thrilled. "Behold, thou art fair, my love; behold, thou art fair; thou hast doves' eyes," he tells her (1:15). "Behold, thou art fair, my beloved, yea, pleasant: also our bed is green," she responds (1:16). Through eight chapters and 117 verses, the two lovers admire each other's physical beauty, expressing their love and devotion.

Day 133

Quotable

- Let him kiss me with the kisses of his mouth: for thy love is better than wine. (1:2)
- He brought me to the banqueting house, and his banner over me was love. (2:4)
- Many waters cannot quench love, neither can the floods drown it. (8:7)

Day 134

Unique and Unusual

Like the book of Esther, Song of Solomon never mentions the name "God."

Day 135

ISAIAH

AUTHOR/DATE

Isaiah, son of Amoz (1:1). Written around 740–700 BC, starting "in the year that king Uzziah died" (6:1).

IN TEN WORDS OR LESS

A coming Messiah will save people from their sins.

Day 136

DETAILS, PLEASE (PART 1)

Like most prophets, Isaiah announced the bad news of punishment for sin. But he also described a coming Messiah who would be "wounded for our transgressions. . .bruised for our iniquities. . .and with his stripes we are healed" (53:5).

Day 137

Details, Please (Part 2)

Called to the ministry through a stunning vision of God in heaven (chapter 6), Isaiah wrote a book that some call "the fifth Gospel" for its predictions of the birth, life, and death of Jesus Christ some seven hundred years later. From Isaiah 9:6, "For unto us a child is born, unto us a son is given: and the government shall be upon his shoulder: and his name shall be called Wonderful, Counsellor, The mighty God, The everlasting Father, The Prince of Peace."

Day 138

Details, Please (Part 3)

Isaiah's prophecies of redemption balance the depressing promises of God's discipline against Judah and Jerusalem, which were overrun by Babylonian armies about a century later. Isaiah's prophecy ends with a long section (chapters 40–66) describing God's restoration of Israel, His promised salvation, and His eternal kingdom.

Day 139

Quotable

- Holy, holy, holy, is the LORD of hosts: the whole earth is full of his glory. (6:3)
- Behold, a virgin shall conceive, and bear a son, and shall call his name Immanuel. (7:14)
- All we like sheep have gone astray; we have turned every one to his own way; and the LORD hath laid on him the iniquity of us all. (53:6)

Day 140

Unique and Unusual

Isaiah had two children with strange, prophetic names. Shear-jashub (7:3) means "a remnant shall return," and Maher-shalal-hash-baz (8:3) means "haste to the spoil." Shear-jashub's name carried God's promise that exiled Jews would one day return home. Maher-shalal-hash-baz's name assured the king of Judah that his country's enemies would be handled by Assyrian armies.

Day 141

JEREMIAH

AUTHORS/DATE

Jeremiah (1:1), with the assistance of Baruch, a
scribe (36:4). Approximately 585 BC.

IN TEN WORDS OR LESS

After years of sinful behavior, Judah will
be punished.

Day 142

DETAILS, PLEASE

Called to the ministry as a boy (1:6), Jeremiah
prophesies bad news to Judah: "Lo, I will bring
a nation upon you from far, O house of Israel,
saith the LORD" (5:15). Jeremiah is mocked for his
prophecies, occasionally beaten, and imprisoned in
a muddy well (chapter 38). But his words come true
with the Babylonian invasion of chapter 52.

Day 143

Quotable

- Behold, as the clay is in the potter's hand, so are ye in mine hand, O house of Israel. (18:6)
- I have loved thee with an everlasting love: therefore with lovingkindness have I drawn thee. (31:3)

---※---

Day 144

Unique and Unusual

The book of Jeremiah that we read is apparently an expanded, second version of a destroyed first draft. King Jehoiakim, angry with Jeremiah for his dire prophecies, cut the scroll with a penknife and "cast it into the fire that was on the hearth" (36:23). At God's command, Jeremiah produced a second scroll with additional material (36:32).

Day 145

LAMENTATIONS

Author/date

Not stated but traditionally attributed to Jeremiah. Probably written around 586 BC, shortly after the fall of Jerusalem to the Babylonians.

In Ten Words or Less

A despairing poem about the destruction of Jerusalem.

Day 146

Details, Please (Part 1)

After warning the southern Jewish nation to obey God, the prophet Jeremiah witnesses the punishment he'd threatened. Judah's "enemies prosper; for the LORD hath afflicted her for the multitude of her transgressions," writes Jeremiah; "her children are gone into captivity before the enemy" (1:5).

Day 147

Details, Please (Part 2)

The sight of the disasters brought on the southern Jewish nation brings tears to Jeremiah's eyes ("Mine eye runneth down with water," 1:16) and provides his nickname, "the weeping prophet." Lamentations ends with a plaintive cry: "Thou hast utterly rejected us; thou art very wroth against us" (5:22).

Day 148

Quotable

- It is of the LORD's mercies that we are not consumed, because his compassions fail not. They are new every morning: great is thy faithfulness. (3:22–23)
- Turn thou us unto thee, O LORD, and we shall be turned; renew our days as of old. (5:21)

Day 149

Unique and Unusual

Though Lamentations doesn't indicate its author, Jeremiah is described in 2 Chronicles as a composer of laments (35:25).

Day 150

EZEKIEL

Author/Date

Ezekiel, a priest (1:1–3). Approximately the 590s–570s BC.

In Ten Words or Less

Though Israel is in exile, the nation will be restored.

Day 151

Details, Please

Ezekiel, an exiled Jew in Babylon, becomes God's spokesman to fellow exiles. He shares unusual (even bizarre) visions with the people, reminding them of the sin that led to their captivity but also offering hope of national restoration.

---※---

Day 152

Quotable

- I have no pleasure in the death of him that dieth, saith the Lord God: wherefore turn yourselves, and live ye. (18:32)
- For thus saith the Lord God; Behold, I, even I, will both search my sheep, and seek them out. As a shepherd seeketh out his flock in the day that he is among this sheep that are scattered; so will I seek out my sheep. (34:11–12)

Day 153

UNIQUE AND UNUSUAL

Ezekiel's vision of a valley of dry bones is one of the Bible's strangest images: "I prophesied as I was commanded: and. . .there was a noise, and behold a shaking, and the bones came together. . . . The sinews and the flesh came up upon them, and the skin covered them above. . . . And the breath came into them, and they lived, and stood up upon their feet, an exceeding great army" (37:7–8, 10).

Day 154

DANIEL

AUTHOR/DATE

Likely Daniel, though some question this. Chapters 7–12 are written in the first person ("I Daniel," 7:15), though the first six chapters are in the third person ("Then Daniel answered," 2:14). Approximately 605–538 BC, during the period of the Babylonian captivity.

IN TEN WORDS OR LESS

Faithful to God in a challenging setting, Daniel is blessed.

Day 155

Details, Please (Part 1)

As a young man, Daniel—along with three others to be known as Shadrach, Meshach, and Abednego— are taken from their home in Jerusalem to serve the king of Babylon. Daniel's God-given ability to interpret dreams endears him to King Nebuchadnezzar.

Day 156

Details, Please (Part 2)

The King's vision of a huge statue, Daniel says, represents existing and future kingdoms. Shadrach, Meshach, and Abednego find trouble when they disobey an order to bow before a statue of Nebuchadnezzar; as punishment, they are thrown into a fiery furnace, where they are protected by an angelic being "like the Son of God" (3:25).

Day 157

DETAILS, PLEASE (PART 3)

The next Babylonian king, Belshazzar, throws a
drinking party using cups stolen from the temple in
Jerusalem; he literally sees "the writing on the wall,"
which Daniel interprets as the soon-to-come take-
over of Babylon by the Medes.

---※---

Day 158

DETAILS, PLEASE (PART 4)

The Median king, Darius, keeps Daniel as an
adviser but is tricked into passing a law designed
by other jealous officials to hurt Daniel, who ends
up in a den of lions. Once again, God protects
His people; Daniel spending a night and replaced
by the schemers, who are mauled by the hungry
beasts. The final six chapters contain Daniel's
prophetic visions, including that of "seventy
weeks" of the end times.

Day 159

Quotable

- Our God whom we serve is able to deliver us from the burning fiery furnace, and he will deliver us out of thine hand, O king. (3:17)
- My God hath sent his angel, and hath shut the lions' mouths, that they have not hurt me. (6:22)
- My God. . .we do not present our supplications before thee for our righteousnesses, but for thy great mercies. (9:18)

Day 160

Unique and Unusual

The book was originally written in two languages: Hebrew (the introduction and most of the prophecies, chapter 1 and chapters 8–12) and Aramaic (the stories of chapters 2–7).

Day 161

HOSEA

Author/Date

Probably Hosea himself, though the text is in both the first and the third person. Written sometime between 750 (approximately when Hosea began ministering) and 722 BC (when Assyria overran Israel).

In Ten Words or Less

Prophet's marriage to prostitute reflects God's relationship with Israel.

Day 162

Details, Please

God gives Hosea a strange command: "Take unto thee a wife of whoredoms" (1:2). The marriage pictures God's relationship to Israel—an honorable, loving husband paired with an unfaithful wife. Hosea marries an adulteress named Gomer and starts a family with her. When Gomer returns to her life of sin, Hosea—again picturing God's faithfulness—buys her back from the slave market. The book contains God's warnings for disobedience but also His promises of blessing for repentance.

Day 163

Quotable

- For they [Israel] have sown the wind, and they shall reap the whirlwind. (8:7)
- The ways of the LORD are right, and the just shall walk in them: but the transgressors shall fall therein. (14:9)

Day 164

Unique and Unusual

Gomer had three children—perhaps Hosea's but maybe not—each given a prophetic name. Son Jezreel was named for a massacre, daughter Lo-ruhamah's name meant "not loved," and son Lo-ammi's name meant "not my people."

Day 165

JOEL

Author/Date

Joel, son of Pethuel (1:1). Little else is known about him. Date unclear but possibly just before the Babylonian invasion of Judah in 586 BC.

In Ten Words or Less

Locust plague pictures God's judgment on His sinful people.

Day 166

Details, Please (part 1)

A devastating locust swarm invades the nation of Judah, but Joel indicates this natural disaster is nothing compared to the coming "great and very terrible" day of the Lord (2:11). God plans to judge His people for sin, but they still have time to repent.

Day 167

Details, Please (part 2)

Obedience to God will bring both physical and spiritual renewal: "I will pour out my spirit upon all flesh," God says (2:28). When the Holy Spirit comes on Christian believers at Pentecost, the apostle Peter quotes this passage to explain what has happened (Acts 2:17).

Day 168

Quotable

- Whosoever shall call on the name of the LORD shall be delivered. (2:32)
- Multitudes, multitudes in the valley of decision: for the day of the LORD is near in the valley of decision. (3:14)

Day 169

UNIQUE AND UNUSUAL

Unlike other prophets who condemned idolatry, injustice, or other specific sins of the Jewish people, Joel simply called for repentance without describing the sin committed.

Day 170

AMOS

AUTHOR/DATE

Amos, a shepherd from Tekoa, near Bethlehem (1:1). Approximately the 760s BC.

IN TEN WORDS OR LESS

Real religion isn't just ritual but treating people with justice.

Day 171

Details, Please (part 1)

An average guy—a lowly shepherd, actually—takes on the rich and powerful of Israelite society, condemning their idol worship, persecution of God's prophets, and cheating of the poor. Though God once rescued the people of Israel from slavery in Egypt, He is ready to send them into new bondage because of their sin.

Day 172

Details, Please (part 2)

Amos sees visions that picture Israel's plight: a plumb line, indicating the people are not measuring up to God's standards, and a basket of ripe fruit, showing the nation is ripe for God's judgment.

Day 173

Quotable

- Prepare to meet thy God, O Israel. (4:12)
- Seek good, and not evil, that ye may live. (5:14)
- Let justice roll down as waters, and righteousness as a mighty stream. (5:24)

Day 174

Unique and Unusual

A native of the southern Jewish kingdom of Judah, Amos was directed by God to prophesy in the northern Jewish nation of Israel.

Day 175

OBADIAH

Author/Date

Obadiah (1), perhaps a person by that name or an unnamed prophet for whom "Obadiah" (meaning "servant of God") is a title. Unclear but probably written within thirty years after Babylon's invasion of Judah in 586 BC.

In Ten Words or Less

Edom will suffer for participating in Jerusalem's destruction.

Day 176

Details, Please (Part 1)

Edom was a nation descended from Esau—twin brother of Jacob, the patriarch of Israel. The baby boys had struggled in their mother's womb (Genesis 25:21–26), and their conflict had continued over the centuries.

Day 177

Details, Please (Part 2)

After Edom took part in the Babylonian ransacking of Jerusalem, Obadiah passed down God's judgment: "For thy violence against thy brother Jacob shame shall cover thee, and thou shalt be cut off for ever" (10).

---※---

Day 178

Quotable

- For the day of the LORD is near upon all the heathen. (15)
- Upon mount Zion shall be deliverance. (17)

DAY 179

UNIQUE AND UNUSUAL

Obadiah is the Old Testament's shortest book—
only one chapter and 21 verses.

---※---

DAY 180

JONAH

AUTHOR/DATE

Unclear; the story is Jonah's but is written in the
third person. Approximately 760 BC. Jonah prophesied during the reign of Israel's King Jeroboam II
(see 2 Kings 14:23–25), who ruled from about 793
to 753 BC.

IN TEN WORDS OR LESS

Reluctant prophet, running from God, is swallowed
by giant fish.

Day 181

DETAILS, PLEASE (PART 1)

God tells Jonah to preach repentance in Nineveh, capital of the brutal Assyrian Empire. Jonah disobeys, sailing in the opposite direction—toward a rendezvous with literary immortality. A storm rocks Jonah's ship, and he spends three days in a giant fish's belly before deciding to obey God after all.

Day 182

DETAILS, PLEASE (PART 2)

When Jonah preaches, Nineveh repents—and God spares the city from the destruction He'd threatened. But the prejudiced Jonah pouts. The story ends with God proclaiming his concern even for vicious pagans.

Day 183

Quotable

- I will pay that that I have vowed. Salvation is of the LORD. (2:9)
- Should not I spare Nineveh, that great city, wherein are more than sixscore thousand persons that cannot discern between their right hand and their left hand? (4:11)

Day 184

Unique and Unusual

Jonah's prophecy didn't come true—because of Nineveh's repentance.

Day 185

MICAH

AUTHOR/DATE

"The word of the LORD that came to Micah the Morasthite" (1:1). Micah either wrote the prophecies or dictated them to another. Approximately 700 BC.

IN TEN WORDS OR LESS

Israel and Judah will suffer for their idolatry and injustice.

Day 186

DETAILS, PLEASE

Micah chastises both the northern and southern Jewish nations for pursuing false gods and cheating the poor. The two nations will be devastated by invaders (the Assyrians), but God will preserve "the remnant of Israel" (2:12).

Day 187

Quotable

- He hath shewed thee, O man, what is good; and what doth the LORD require of thee, but to do justly, and to love mercy, and to walk humbly with thy God? (6:8)

Day 188

Unique and Unusual

Centuries before Jesus' birth, Micah predicted the town where it would occur: "But thou, Bethlehem Ephratah, though thou be little among the thousands of Judah, yet out of thee shall he come forth unto me that is to be ruler in Israel" (5:2).

Day 189

NAHUM

Author/Date

"The book of the vision of Nahum the Elkoshite" (1:1). Nahum either wrote the prophecies or dictated them to another. Sometime between 663 and 612 BC.

In Ten Words or Less

Powerful, wicked Nineveh will fall before God's judgment.

---✻---

Day 190

Details, Please

"Woe to the bloody city!" Nahum cries (3:1). Nineveh, capital of the brutal Assyrian Empire, has been targeted for judgment by God Himself, who will "make thee vile, and will set thee as a gazingstock" (3:6) for sins of idolatry and cruelty. Nahum's prophecy comes true when the Babylonian Empire overruns Nineveh in 612 BC.

Day 191

Quotable

- The LORD is slow to anger, and great in power, and will not at all acquit the wicked. (1:3)
- The LORD is good, a strong hold in the day of trouble; and he knoweth them that trust in him. (1:7)

Day 192

Unique and Unusual

Nahum is a kind of Jonah, part 2. Though the city had once avoided God's judgment by taking Jonah's preaching to heart and repenting, now, more than a century later, it will experience the full consequence of its sins.

Day 193

HABAKKUK

Author/Date

Habakkuk (1:1); nothing is known of his background. Approximately 600 BC.

In Ten Words or Less

Trust God even when He seems unresponsive or unfair.

Day 194

Details, Please (Part 1)

In Judah, a prophet complains that God allows violence and injustice among His people. But Habakkuk is shocked to learn the Lord's plan for dealing with the problem: sending the "bitter and hasty" (1:6) Chaldeans to punish Judah.

Day 195

Details, Please (Part 2)

Habakkuk argues that the Chaldeans are far worse than the disobedient Jews, telling God, "Thou art of purer eyes than to behold evil" (1:13). The Lord, however, says He's only using the Chaldeans for His purposes and will in time punish them for their own sins.

---※---

Day 196

Details, Please (Part 3)

It's not Habakkuk's job to question God's ways: "The LORD is in his holy temple: let all the earth keep silence before him" (2:20). Habakkuk, like Job, ultimately submits to God's authority.

Day 197

Quotable

- The just shall live by his faith. (2:4)
- I will joy in the God of my salvation. (3:18)

—————————✳—————————

Day 198

Unique and Unusual

The apostle Paul quotes Habakkuk 2:4 in his powerful Gospel presentation in Romans 1.

Day 199

ZEPHANIAH

Author/Date
Zephaniah (1:1). Approximately 640–620 BC, during the reign of King Josiah (1:1).

In Ten Words or Less
A coming "day of the Lord" promises heavy judgment.

Day 200

Details, Please (Part 1)
Zephaniah begins with a jarring prophecy: "I will utterly consume all things from off the land," God declares in the book's second verse. People, animals, birds, and fish will all perish, victims of God's wrath over Judah's idolatry.

Day 201

DETAILS, PLEASE (PART 2)

Other nearby nations will be punished as well, in "the fire of my jealousy" (3:8), but there is hope: In His mercy, God will one day restore a remnant of Israel that "shall not do iniquity, nor speak lies" (3:13).

Day 202

QUOTABLE

- The great day of the LORD is near. . .and hasteth greatly. (1:14)
- The LORD thy God in the midst of thee is mighty; he will save, he will rejoice over thee with joy. (3:17)

Day 203

Unique and Unusual

Zephaniah gives more detail about himself than most of the minor prophets, identifying himself as a great-great-grandson of Hezekiah (1:1), probably the popular, godly king of Judah (2 Chronicles 29).

Day 204

HAGGAI

Author/Date

Haggai (1:1). 520 BC—a precise date because Haggai mentions "the second year of Darius the king" (1:1), which can be verified against Persian records.

In Ten Words or Less

Jews returning from exile need to rebuild God's temple.

Day 205

DETAILS, PLEASE

One of three "postexilic" prophets, Haggai encourages former Babylonian captives to restore the demolished temple in Jerusalem. The new world power, Persia, has allowed the people to return to Jerusalem, but the people have become distracted with building their own comfortable homes. Through Haggai, God tells the people to rebuild the temple first in order to break a drought that's affecting the countryside.

Day 206

QUOTABLE

- Be strong, all ye people of the land, saith the LORD, and work: for I am with you, saith the LORD of hosts. (2:4)

Day 207

Unique and Unusual

Haggai seems to hint at the end-times tribulation and second coming of Christ when he quotes God as saying, "I will shake the heavens, and the earth, and the sea, and the dry land; and I will shake all nations, and the desire of all nations shall come" (2:6–7).

Day 208

ZECHARIAH

Author/Date

Zechariah, son of Berechiah (1:1); some believe a second, unnamed writer contributed chapters 9–14. Approximately 520–475 BC.

In Ten Words or Less

Jewish exiles should rebuild their temple—and anticipate their Messiah.

Day 209

Details, Please (Part 1)

Like Haggai, another postexilic prophet, Zechariah urges Jewish people to rebuild the Jerusalem temple. He also gives several prophecies of the coming Messiah, including an end-times vision of a final battle over Jerusalem.

Day 210

Details, Please (Part 2)

In that final battle over Jerusalem, "the LORD [shall] go forth, and fight against those nations. . . . And his feet shall stand in that day upon the mount of Olives. . . . And the LORD shall be king over all the earth" (14:3–4, 9).

Day 211

Quotable

- Turn ye unto me, saith the LORD of hosts, and I will turn unto you. (1:3)

Day 212

Unique and Unusual

Zechariah's prophecy of the Messiah riding a donkey into Jerusalem (9:9) was fulfilled to the letter in Jesus' "triumphal entry" (Matthew 21:1–11). The prophecy "They shall look upon me whom they have pierced" (12:10) refers to the Roman soldiers' spearing of Christ after the crucifixion (John 19:34).

Day 213

MALACHI

AUTHOR

Malachi (1:1), meaning "my messenger." No other details are given. Approximately 450 BC.

IN TEN WORDS OR LESS

The Jews have become careless in their attitude toward God.

Day 214

DETAILS, PLEASE (PART 1)

Prophesying a century after the return from exile, Malachi chastises the Jews for offering "lame and sick" sacrifices (1:8); for divorcing their wives to marry pagan women (2:11, 14); and for failing to pay tithes for the temple (3:8).

Day 215

Details, Please (Part 2)

The Lord was angry with the attitude "It is vain to serve God" (3:14), but He promised to bless the obedient: "Unto you that fear my name shall the Sun of righteousness arise with healing in his wings" (4:2).

---※---

Day 216

Quotable

- For I am the Lord, I change not. (3:6)
- Return unto me, and I will return unto you, saith the Lord of hosts. (3:7)

Day 217

UNIQUE AND UNUSUAL

Malachi, the last book of the Old Testament, contains the final word from God for some four hundred years, until the appearance of John the Baptist and Jesus, the Messiah, as prophesied in Malachi 3:1: "I will send my messenger, and he shall prepare the way before me, and the LORD, whom ye seek, shall suddenly come to his temple."

Day 218

MATTHEW

AUTHOR/DATE

Not stated but traditionally attributed to Matthew, a tax collector (9:9). Matthew is also known as "Levi" (Mark 2:14). Approximately AD 70, when Romans destroyed the temple in Jerusalem.

IN TEN WORDS OR LESS

Jesus fulfills the Old Testament prophecies of a coming Messiah.

Day 219

Details, Please (Part 1)

The first of the four *Gospels* (meaning "good news"), the book of Matthew ties what follows in the New Testament to what came before in the Old. The book, written primarily to a Jewish audience, uses numerous Old Testament references to prove that Jesus is the promised Messiah the Jews have been anticipating for centuries.

Day 220

Details, Please (Part 2)

He ties the Old Testament to the New by beginning with a genealogy that shows Jesus' ancestry through King David and the patriarch Abraham. Matthew then details the angelic announcement of Jesus' conception and the visit of the "wise men" with their gifts of gold, frankincense, and myrrh.

Day 221

Details, Please (Part 3)

Matthew introduces the character of John the Baptist, relative and forerunner of Jesus, and describes the calling of key disciples Peter, Andrew, James, and John. Jesus' teachings are emphasized, with long passages covering His Sermon on the Mount (chapters 5–7), including the Beatitudes ("Blessed are they. . .") and the Lord's Prayer ("Our Father, which art in heaven. . .").

Day 222

Details, Please (Part 4)

As with all four Gospels, Matthew also details the death, burial, and resurrection of Jesus and is the only biographer of Jesus to mention several miracles—the tearing of the temple curtain, an earthquake, the breaking open of tombs, and the raising to life of dead saints—that occurred during that time (27:50–54).

Day 223

Quotable (Part 1)

- She shall bring forth a son, and thou shalt call his name JESUS: for he shall save his people from their sins. (1:21)
- Ye are the salt of the earth. . . . Ye are the light of the world. (5:13–14)
- Love your enemies, bless them that curse you, do good to them that hate you, and pray for them which despitefully use you, and persecute you. (5:44)

Day 224

Quotable (Part 2)

- Judge not, that ye be not judged. (7:1)
- Ask, and it shall be given you; seek, and ye shall find; knock, and it shall be opened unto you. (7:7)
- Go ye therefore, and teach all nations, baptizing them in the name of the Father, and of the Son, and of the Holy Ghost. (28:19)

Day 225

Unique and Unusual

Matthew is the only Gospel to use the terms "church" and "kingdom of heaven."

Day 226

MARK

Author/Date

Not stated but traditionally attributed to John Mark, a missionary companion of Paul and Barnabas (Acts 12:25) and an associate of the apostle Peter (1 Peter 5:13). Probably AD 60s, during the Roman persecution of Christians.

In Ten Words or Less

Jesus is God's Son, a suffering servant of all people.

Day 227

Details, Please (Part 1)

The second of the four Gospels is believed by most scholars to be the first one written. The book of Mark is the briefest and most active of the four biographies of Jesus, the majority of which is repeated in the Gospels of Matthew and Luke.

Day 228

Details, Please (Part 2)

Mark addresses a Gentile audience, portraying Jesus as a man of action, divinely capable of healing the sick, controlling nature, and battling the powers of Satan. Mark's theme of the suffering servant comes through in his narratives of Jesus' interaction with hostile doubters—the Jewish leaders, who want to kill Him (9:31); His neighbors, who take offense at Him (6:3); and even His own family members, who think He's crazy (3:21).

Day 229

DETAILS, PLEASE (PART 3)

The abasement of Jesus pictures what His disciples should pursue: "Whosoever will be great among you, shall be your minister: and whosoever of you will be the chiefest, shall be servant of all. For even the Son of man came not to be ministered unto, but to minister, and to give his life a ransom for many" (10:43–45).

Day 230

QUOTABLE (PART 1)

- Come ye after me, and I will make you to become fishers of men. (1:17)
- Suffer the little children to come unto me, and forbid them not: for of such is the kingdom of God. (10:14)
- It is easier for a camel to go through the eye of a needle, than for a rich man to enter into the kingdom of God. (10:25)

Day 231

Quotable (Part 2)

- Render to Caesar the things that are Caesar's, and to God the things that are God's. (12:17)
- Watch ye and pray, lest ye enter into temptation. The spirit truly is ready, but the flesh is weak. (14:38)

Day 232

Unique and Unusual

Many believe an unnamed spectator at Jesus' arrest, mentioned in Mark's Gospel, was Mark himself: "And there followed him a certain young man, having a linen cloth cast about his naked body; and the young men laid hold on him: and he left the linen cloth, and fled from them naked" (14:51–52).

Day 233

LUKE

Author/Date

Not stated but traditionally attributed to Luke, a Gentile physician (Colossians 4:14) and a missionary companion of the apostle Paul (2 Timothy 4:11). Possibly written during the AD 70s–80s, as the Gospel was spreading throughout the Roman Empire.

In Ten Words or Less

Jesus is Savior of all people, whether Jew or Gentile.

Day 234

Details, Please (Part 1)

Luke's Gospel is addressed to a man named Theophilus (1:3), "to set forth in order a declaration of those things which are most surely believed among us" about Jesus Christ (1:1). It's unclear who Theophilus was, though some believe he may have been a Roman official.

Day 235

DETAILS, PLEASE (PART 2)

Luke's book is the least Jewish and most universal of the four Gospels. Luke traces Jesus' genealogy beyond Abraham, the patriarch of the Jews, all the way back to Adam, "the son of God" (3:38), common ancestor of everyone.

Day 236

DETAILS, PLEASE (PART 3)

Luke also shows Jesus' compassion for all people: Roman soldiers (7:1–10), widows (7:11–17), the "sinful" (7:36–50), the chronically ill (8:43–48), lepers (17:11–19), and many others—including a criminal condemned to die on a cross beside Jesus (23:40–43).

Day 237

Details, Please (Part 4)

As with all the Gospels, Luke shows Jesus' resurrection, adding detailed accounts of His appearances to two believers on the Emmaus road and the remaining eleven disciples. As the Gospel ends, Jesus is ascending into heaven—setting the stage for a sequel of sorts, Luke's book of Acts.

Day 238

Quotable (Part 1)

- For where your treasure is, there will your heart be also. (12:34)
- I say unto you, that likewise joy shall be in heaven over one sinner that repenteth, more than over ninety and nine just persons, which need no repentance. (15:7)

Day 239

Quotable (Part 2)

- Whosoever shall seek to save his life shall lose it; and whosoever shall lose his life shall preserve it. (17:33)
- Whosoever shall not receive the kingdom of God as a little child shall in no wise enter therein. (18:17)
- For the Son of man is come to seek and to save that which was lost. (19:10)

Day 240

Unique and Unusual

Luke is the only Gospel to share Jesus' stories ("parables") of the good Samaritan (10:25–37), the prodigal son (15:11–32), and the rich man and Lazarus (16:19–31). Luke is also the only Gospel to detail Jesus' actual birth and words He spoke in childhood (both in chapter 2).

Day 241

JOHN

Author/Date

Not stated but traditionally attributed to John, the "disciple whom Jesus loved" (John 21:7), brother of James and son of Zebedee (Matthew 4:21). Around the AD 90s, as the last Gospel written.

In Ten Words or Less

Jesus is God Himself, the only Savior of the world.

Day 242

Details, Please (Part 1)

While the books of Matthew, Mark, and Luke have many similarities (they're called the "synoptic Gospels," meaning they take a common view), the book of John stands alone. The fourth Gospel downplays Jesus' parables (none are recorded) and miracles (only seven are featured).

Day 243

Details, Please (Part 2)

Instead, John provides more extensive treatments of Jesus' reasons for coming to earth ("I am come that they might have life, and that they might have it more abundantly," 10:10); His intimate relationship with God the Father ("I and my Father are one," 10:30).

Day 244

Details, Please (Part 3)

John also records Jesus' own feelings toward the job He had come to do ("Father, the hour is come; glorify thy Son, that thy Son also may glorify thee: as thou hast given him power over all flesh, that he should give eternal life to as many as thou hast given him," 17:1–2). John also gives special emphasis to Jesus' patient treatment of the disciples Thomas, who doubted the resurrection (20:24–29), and Peter, who had denied the Lord (21:15–23).

Day 245

Quotable (Part 1)

- In the beginning was the Word, and the Word was with God, and the Word was God. (1:1)
- For God so loved the world, that he gave his only begotten Son, that whosoever believeth in him should not perish, but have everlasting life. (3:16)

Day 246

Quotable (Part 2)

- I am the bread of life. (6:35)
- I am the good shepherd: the good shepherd giveth his life for the sheep. (10:11)
- I am the way, the truth, and the life: no man cometh unto the Father, but by me. (14:6)

Day 247

Unique and Unusual

Jesus' very first miracle, His changing of water into wine at a wedding in Cana, is recorded only in John's Gospel (2:1–12). So is His raising of Lazarus from the dead (11:1–44), His healing of a man born blind (9:1–38), and His long-distance healing of a nobleman's son (4:46–54). John is also the only Gospel to mention Nicodemus, who heard Jesus' teaching that "ye must be born again" (3:7).

Day 248

ACTS

Author/Date

Not stated but traditionally attributed to Luke, a Gentile physician (Colossians 4:14), a missionary companion of the apostle Paul (2 Timothy 4:11), and the author of the Gospel of Luke. Covering events of the AD 30s–60s, Acts was probably written sometime between AD 62 and 80.

In Ten Words or Less

The Holy Spirit's arrival heralds the beginning of Christian church.

Day 249

Details, Please (Part 1)

Officially called "Acts of the Apostles," the book of
Acts is a bridge between the story of Jesus in the
Gospels and the life of the church in the letters
that follow. Luke begins with Jesus' ascension into
heaven after forty days of post-resurrection activity,
"speaking of the things pertaining to the kingdom
of God" (1:3).

Day 250

Details, Please (Part 2)

Ten days after Jesus' ascension into heaven,
God sends the Holy Spirit on the festival day of
Pentecost—and the church is born. Through the
Spirit, the disciples are empowered to preach boldly
about Jesus, and three thousand people become
Christians that day. Jewish leaders, fearing the new
movement called "this way" (9:2), begin persecuting
believers, who scatter to other areas and spread the
Gospel through much of the known world.

Day 251

Details, Please (Part 3)

The ultimate persecutor, Saul, becomes a Christian himself after meeting the brightly shining, heavenly Jesus on the road to Damascus. Saul, later called Paul, ultimately joins Peter and other Christian leaders in preaching, working miracles, and strengthening the fledgling church.

Day 252

Quotable (Part 1)

- Ye men of Galilee, why stand ye gazing up into heaven? this same Jesus, which is taken up from you into heaven, shall so come in like manner as ye have seen him go into heaven. (1:11)
- Repent, and be baptized every one of you in the name of Jesus Christ for the remission of sins, and ye shall receive the gift of the Holy Ghost. (2:38)

Day 253

Quotable (Part 2)

- Neither is there salvation in any other: for there is none other name under heaven given among men, whereby we must be saved. (4:12)
- Saul, Saul, why persecutest thou me? (9:4)

Day 254

Unique and Unusual

Acts tells of the first Christian martyr, Stephen, stoned to death for blaming Jewish leaders for the death of Jesus (chapter 7). Acts also depicts the Gospel's transition from a purely Jewish message to one for all people (9:15; 10:45) and the beginning of the Christian missionary movement (chapter 13).

Day 255

ROMANS

AUTHORS/DATE

The apostle Paul (1:1), with the secretarial assistance of Tertius (16:22). Approximately AD 57, near the conclusion of Paul's third missionary journey.

IN TEN WORDS OR LESS

Sinners are saved only by faith in Jesus Christ.

Day 256

DETAILS, PLEASE (PART 1)

Some call Romans a "theology textbook" for its thorough explanation of the Christian life. Paul begins by describing God's righteous anger against human sin (chapters 1–2), noting that everyone falls short of God's standard (3:23).

Day 257

Details, Please (Part 2)

But God Himself provides the only way to overcome that sin, "the righteousness of God which is by faith of Jesus Christ unto all and upon all them that believe" (3:22). Being justified (made right) through faith in Jesus, we can consider ourselves "to be dead indeed unto sin, but alive unto God through Jesus Christ our Lord" (6:11).

Day 258

Details, Please (Part 3)

God's Spirit will "quicken" (give life to, 8:11) all who believe in Jesus, allowing us to "present [our] bodies a living sacrifice, holy, acceptable unto God" (12:1). It is possible, with God's help, to "be not overcome of evil, but [to] overcome evil with good" (12:21).

Day 259

Quotable (Part 1)

- All have sinned, and come short of the glory of God. (3:23)
- God commendeth his love toward us, in that, while we were yet sinners, Christ died for us. (5:8)
- The wages of sin is death; but the gift of God is eternal life through Jesus Christ our Lord. (6:23)

Day 260

Quotable (Part 2)

- We know that all things work together for good to them that love God, to them who are the called according to his purpose. (8:28)
- Owe no man any thing, but to love one another: for he that loveth another hath fulfilled the law. (13:8)
- Love worketh no ill to his neighbour: therefore love is the fulfilling of the law. (13:10)

Day 261

Unique and Unusual

Unlike Paul's other letters to churches, Romans was addressed to a congregation he'd never met. The great missionary was hoping to see the Roman Christians personally while traveling westward to Spain (15:23–24). It's unclear if Paul ever actually reached Spain or if he was executed in Rome after the end of the book of Acts.

Day 262

1 CORINTHIANS

Authors/Date

The apostle Paul, with the assistance of Sosthenes (1:1). Approximately AD 55–57.

In Ten Words or Less

An apostle tackles sin problems in the church at Corinth.

Day 263

DETAILS, PLEASE (PART 1)

Paul had helped found the church in Corinth (Acts 18) but then moved on to other mission fields. While in Ephesus, he learns of serious problems in the Corinthian congregation and writes a long letter to address those issues.

Day 264

DETAILS, PLEASE (PART 2)

For those arguing over who should lead the church, Paul urges "that ye be perfectly joined together in the same mind and in the same judgment" (1:10). For a man involved in an immoral relationship with his stepmother, Paul commands, "Put away from among yourselves that wicked person" (5:13).

Day 265

Details, Please (Part 3)

For those church members filing lawsuits against others, Paul warns, "Know ye not that the unrighteous shall not inherit the kingdom of God?" (6:9). The apostle also teaches on marriage, Christian liberty, the Lord's Supper, spiritual gifts, and the resurrection of the dead. In the famous thirteenth chapter of 1 Corinthians, Paul describes the "more excellent way" (12:31): that of charity, or love.

Day 266

Quotable (Part 1)

- For the preaching of the cross is to them that perish foolishness; but unto us which are saved it is the power of God. (1:18)
- The foolishness of God is wiser than men; and the weakness of God is stronger than men. (1:25)
- For other foundation can no man lay than that is laid, which is Jesus Christ. (3:11)

Day 267

Quotable (Part 2)

- I am made all things to all men, that I might by all means save some. (9:22)
- For as often as ye eat this bread, and drink this cup, ye do shew the Lord's death till he come. (11:26)
- Though I speak with the tongues of men and of angels, and have not charity, I am become as sounding brass, or a tinkling cymbal. (13:1)

Day 268

Unique and Unusual

Refuting opponents who questioned his apostleship, Paul insists that he is as much an apostle as Jesus' original disciples. "Am I am not an apostle?" he asks in 1 Corinthians 9:1. "Have I not seen Jesus Christ our Lord?"

Day 269

2 CORINTHIANS

Authors/Date

The apostle Paul, with Timothy's assistance (1:1). Approximately AD 55–57, shortly after the writing of 1 Corinthians.

In Ten Words or Less

Paul defends his ministry to the troubled Corinthian church.

Day 270

Details, Please (Part 1)

Corinthian believers had apparently addressed some of the problems Paul's first letter mentioned— though there were still troublemakers who questioned his authority. He was forced to "speak foolishly" (11:21), boasting of hardships he'd faced serving Jesus: "in labours more abundant, in stripes above measure, in prisons more frequent, in deaths oft" (11:23).

Day 271

Details, Please (Part 2)

Paul even suffered a "thorn in the flesh" (12:7), which God refused to take away, telling him instead, "My grace is sufficient for thee: for my strength is made perfect in weakness" (12:9). His parting warning: "Examine yourselves, whether ye be in the faith; prove your own selves" (13:5).

---※---

Day 272

Quotable

- We have this treasure in earthen vessels, that the excellence of the power may be of God, and not of us. (4:7)
- For he hath made him to be sin for us, who knew no sin; that we might be made the righteousness of God in him. (5:21)
- God loveth a cheerful giver. (9:7)

Day 273

Unique and Unusual

Paul never identifies his "thorn in the flesh," though some speculate it may have been bad eyesight, temptations, even physical unattractiveness.

Day 274

GALATIANS

Author/Date

The apostle Paul (1:1). Perhaps written around AD 49, as one of Paul's earliest letters.

In Ten Words or Less

Christians are free from restrictive Jewish laws.

Day 275

DETAILS, PLEASE (PART 1)

Writing to several regional churches, Paul can only "marvel" (1:6) that Galatian Christians have turned from their freedom in Jesus back to the rules of Old Testament Judaism. Some people tried to compel Christians "to live as do the Jews" (2:14).

---※---

Day 276

DETAILS, PLEASE (PART 2)

Compelling Christians to live under the Old Testament law was an error even the apostle Peter made (2:11–13). Paul argued strongly "that no man is justified by the law in the sight of God. . .for, The just shall live by faith" (3:11).

Day 277

Quotable

- O foolish Galatians, who hath bewitched you? (3:1)
- The fruit of the Spirit is love, joy, peace, long-suffering, gentleness, goodness, faith, meekness, temperance: against such there is no law. (5:22–23)

Day 278

Unique and Unusual

One of Paul's closing comments, "Ye see how large a letter I have written unto you with mine own hand" (6:11), makes some believe that poor eyesight was the apostle's "thorn in the flesh" (2 Corinthians 12:7).

Day 279

EPHESIANS

Author/Date

The apostle Paul (1:1). Around AD 62, toward the end of Paul's life.

In Ten Words or Less

Christians are all members of Jesus' "body," the church.

Day 280

Details, Please

Paul had started the church in Ephesus (Acts 19) and now explains in detail the church members' relationship to Jesus Christ—so that they "may grow up into him in all things, which is the head, even Christ" (4:15). Through Jesus, God has reconciled both Jews and Gentiles to Himself (2:11–18). This new life should result in pure, honest living in the church and in the home (chapters 4–6).

Day 281

Quotable

- By grace are ye saved through faith; and that not of yourselves: it is the gift of God: not of works, lest any man should boast. (2:8–9)
- Put on the whole armour of God, that ye may be able to stand against the wiles of the devil. (6:11)

Day 282

Unique and Unusual

Paul tells servants (slaves, in today's language) to "be obedient to them that are your masters" (6:5). Why? Because God will reward such behavior (6:8).

Day 283

PHILIPPIANS

AUTHORS/DATE

The apostle Paul, along with Timothy (1:1). Probably the early 60s AD

IN TEN WORDS OR LESS

"Friendship letter" between the apostle Paul and a beloved church.

Day 284

DETAILS, PLEASE

With sixteen references to "joy" and "rejoicing," Philippians is one of the apostle Paul's most upbeat letters—even though he wrote it in "bonds" (1:13). Paul thanks the church at Philippi for its support (1:3–5) and encourages its people to "rejoice in the Lord always: and again I say, Rejoice" (4:4).

DAY 285

QUOTABLE

- For to me to live is Christ, and to die is gain. (1:21)
- I press toward the mark for the prize of the high calling of God in Christ Jesus. (3:14)
- Be careful for nothing; but in every thing by prayer and supplication with thanksgiving let your requests be made known unto God. (4:6)

DAY 286

UNIQUE AND UNUSUAL

Though unity is a common theme in Paul's letters, he singles out two Philippian women, Euodias and Syntyche, pleading that they "be of the same mind in the Lord" (4:2).

Day 287

COLOSSIANS

Authors/Date

The apostle Paul, along with Timothy (1:1). Probably the early 60s AD

In Ten Words or Less

Jesus Christ is supreme—over everyone and everything.

Day 288

Details, Please

False teaching ("enticing words," 2:4) had infiltrated the church at Colosse, apparently causing some people to add unnecessary and unhelpful elements to their Christian faith. Paul sent this letter to remind Christians of the superiority of Jesus over Jewish rules and regulations (2:16), angels (2:18), and anything else. Jesus is "the image of the invisible God, the firstborn of every creature" (1:15).

Day 289

QUOTABLE

- For this cause we also, since the day we heard it, do not cease to pray for you. (1:9)
- Set your affection on things above, not on things on the earth. (3:2)
- Let the peace of God rule in your hearts, to the which also ye are called in one body; and be ye thankful. (3:15)

Day 290

UNIQUE AND UNUSUAL

Paul mentions a letter to Laodicea (4:16) that apparently did not make the cut as New Testament scripture.

Day 291

1 THESSALONIANS

Authors/Date

The apostle Paul, along with Silvanus (Silas) and Timothy (1:1). The early 50s AD—perhaps Paul's earliest letter.

In Ten Words or Less

Jesus will return to gather His followers to Him.

Day 292

Details, Please

In this letter to another church he helped found (see Acts 17), Paul teaches on the second coming of Christ, apparently an issue of some concern to the Thessalonians. Paul describes *how* Jesus will return but doesn't say exactly *when*. The important thing, in his words, is "that ye would walk worthy of God, who hath called you unto his kingdom and glory" (2:12).

Day 293

Quotable

- For the Lord himself shall descend from heaven with a shout, with the voice of the archangel, and with the trump of God: and the dead in Christ shall rise first. (4:16)
- The day of the Lord so cometh as a thief in the night. (5:2)

Day 294

Unique and Unusual

First Thessalonians contains two of the Bible's shortest verses: "Rejoice evermore" (5:16) and "Pray without ceasing" (5:17).

Day 295

2 THESSALONIANS

Authors/Date

The apostle Paul, along with Silvanus (Silas) and Timothy (1:1). The early 50s AD—perhaps Paul's second-oldest letter.

In Ten Words or Less

Christians should work until Jesus returns.

Day 296

Details, Please (Part 1)

Shortly after writing 1 Thessalonians, Paul dictates a follow-up. Apparently, a letter falsely claiming to be from Paul had left the Thessalonians "shaken in mind. . .troubled" (2:2) at the thought that Jesus had already returned.

Day 297

Details, Please (Part 2)

Paul assures them that the event of Jesus' return is still a future event—and urges everyone to live positive and productive lives until the second coming. "If any would not work," Paul commands those who have dropped out in anticipation of Jesus' return, "neither should he eat" (3:10).

Day 298

Quotable

- You who are troubled rest with us, when the Lord Jesus shall be revealed from heaven with his mighty angels. (1:7)
- Brethren, be not weary in well doing. (3:13)

Day 299

Unique and Unusual

The fact that Paul dictated this letter is clear from his comment "The salutation of Paul with mine own hand. . .so I write" (3:17).

Day 300

1 TIMOTHY

Author/Date

The apostle Paul (1:1). Approximately AD 63.

In Ten Words or Less

Pastors are taught how to conduct their lives and churches.

Day 301

Details, Please

The first of three "pastoral epistles," 1 Timothy contains the aging apostle Paul's insights for a new generation of church leaders. Timothy had often worked alongside Paul but was now pastoring in Ephesus (1:3). Paul warned him against legalism and false teaching (chapter 1), listed the qualifications for pastors and deacons (chapter 3), and described the behavior of a "good minister of Jesus Christ" (4:6) in the final three chapters.

Day 302

Quotable

- Christ Jesus came into the world to save sinners; of whom I am chief. (1:15)
- This is a true saying, If a man desire the office of a bishop, he desireth a good work. (3:1)

Day 303

Unique and Unusual

First Timothy seems to command good pay for pastors: "Let the elders that rule well be counted worthy of double honour. . . . The labourer is worthy of his reward" (5:17–18).

Day 304

2 TIMOTHY

Author/Date

The apostle Paul (1:1). Probably the mid-60s AD.

In Ten Words or Less

The apostle Paul's final words to a beloved coworker.

Day 305

Details, Please (Part 1)

Second Timothy may be the last known letter of Paul. Addressed to "Timothy, my dearly beloved son" (1:2), the book warns the young pastor against false teaching and urges him to live a life of purity before his congregation.

Day 306

Details, Please (Part 2)

Paul tells Timothy that he should expect trouble ("All that will live godly in Christ Jesus shall suffer persecution," 3:12), but God will be faithful ("The Lord shall deliver me from every evil work, and will preserve me unto his heavenly kingdom," 4:18). Paul begs Timothy to join him as quickly as possible, as "the time of my departure is at hand" (4:6).

Day 307

Quotable

- This know also, that in the last days perilous times shall come. (3:1)
- Thou therefore endure hardness, as a good soldier of Jesus Christ. (2:3)
- Preach the word; be instant in season, out of season; reprove, rebuke, exhort with all long suffering and doctrine. (4:2)

---※---

Day 308

Unique and Unusual

Paul tells where the Bible comes from in 2 Timothy: "All scripture is given by inspiration of God" (3:16). The idea of the word *inspiration* is "breathed out."

Day 309

TITUS

Author/Date

The apostle Paul (1:1). Approximately AD 63.

In Ten Words or Less

Church leaders are instructed on their lives and teaching.

———————✳———————

Day 310

Details, Please (Part 1)

On the Mediterranean island of Crete, Paul left Titus to "set in order the things that are wanting, and ordain elders" (1:5) for the fledgling church. The people of Crete were known for their poor behavior (see "Unique and Unusual" on Day 313).

Day 311

Details, Please (Part 2)

The untrustworthy people of Crete needed the kind of church leader who holds fast to "the faithful word as he hath been taught, that he may be able by sound doctrine both to exhort and to convince the gainsayers" (1:9).

Day 312

Quotable

- Looking for that blessed hope, and the glorious appearing of the great God and our Saviour Jesus Christ. (2:13)
- Not by works of righteousness which we have done, but according to his mercy he saved us, by the washing of regeneration, and renewing of the Holy Ghost. (3:5)

Day 313

Unique and Unusual

Paul quotes a Cretan philosopher in this letter: "One of themselves, even a prophet of their own, said, The Cretians are alway liars, evil beasts, slow bellies" (1:12). The quotation is from Epimenides, of the sixth century BC.

Day 314

PHILEMON

Authors/Date

The apostle Paul, along with Timothy (1). Probably around AD 63, when Paul was imprisoned in Rome.

In Ten Words or Less

Paul begs mercy for a runaway slave converted to Christianity.

Day 315

Details, Please (Part 1)

Philemon is a "fellowlabourer" (1) of Paul, a man who has "refreshed" (7) other Christians with his love and generosity. But the apostle writes with a deeper request—that Philemon forgive and take back a runaway slave.

Day 316

Details, Please (Part 2)

The runaway slave had apparently accepted Christ under Paul's teaching: "my son Onesimus, whom I have begotten in my bonds" (10). "If thou count me therefore a partner," Paul wrote to Philemon, "receive him as myself" (17).

Day 317

Quotable

- I thank my God, making mention of thee always in my prayers, hearing of thy love and faith, which thou hast toward the Lord Jesus, and toward all saints. (4–5)
- Having confidence in thy obedience I wrote unto thee, knowing that thou wilt also do more than I say. (21)

Day 318

Unique and Unusual

With only one chapter and twenty-five verses, Philemon is the shortest of Paul's letters in the Bible.

Day 319

HEBREWS

Author/Date

Not stated; Paul, Luke, Barnabas, and Apollos have all been suggested. Probably written sometime before AD 70, since Hebrews refers to temple sacrifices. The Jerusalem temple was destroyed by Romans in AD 70.

In Ten Words or Less

Jesus is better than any Old Testament person or sacrifice.

Day 320

Details, Please (Part 1)

Written to Jewish Christians (hence the name "Hebrews"), this long letter emphasizes the superiority of Christianity to Old Testament Judaism. Jesus is "so much better" (1:4) than angels, Moses, and the previous animal sacrifices.

Day 321

DETAILS, PLEASE (PART 2)

In showing the superiority of Jesus, Hebrews asks, "For if the blood of bulls and of goats, and the ashes of an heifer sprinkling the unclean, sanctifieth to the purifying of the flesh: how much more shall the blood of Christ, who through the eternal Spirit offered himself without spot to God, purge your conscience from dead works to serve the living God?" (9:13–14).

Day 322

DETAILS, PLEASE (PART 3)

Jewish Christians, some of whom were apparently wavering in their commitment to Jesus, are reminded that Christ "is the mediator of a better covenant, which was established upon better promises" (8:6)—a once-for-all sacrifice on the cross that provides "eternal redemption for us" (9:12).

Day 323

Quotable (Part 1)

- How shall we escape, if we neglect so great salvation. (2:3)
- There remaineth therefore a rest to the people of God. (4:9)
- It is appointed unto men once to die, but after this the judgment. (9:27)

Day 324

Quotable (Part 2)

- Not forsaking the assembling of ourselves together, as the manner of some is; but exhorting one another: and so much the more, as ye see the day approaching. (10:25)
- Now faith is the substance of things hoped for, the evidence of things not seen. (11:1)

Day 325

Quotable (Part 3)

- Wherefore seeing we also are compassed about with so great a cloud of witnesses, let us lay aside every weight, and the sin which doth so easily beset us, and let us run with patience the race that is set before us, looking unto Jesus the author and finisher of our faith. (12:1–2)
- Let brotherly love continue. (13:1)

Day 326

Unique and Unusual

Hebrews is one of only two New Testament letters (the other being 1 John) that includes no greeting or hint of its author.

Day 327

JAMES

Author/Date

James (1:1), probably a brother of Jesus (see Matthew 13:55; Mark 6:3). Approximately AD 60.

In Ten Words or Less

Real Christian faith is shown by one's good works.

---※---

Day 328

Details, Please (Part 1)

Though the apostle Paul clearly taught that salvation is by faith alone and not by good works (see Romans 3:28), James clarifies that good works will *follow* true faith: "What doth it profit, my brethren, though a man say he hath faith, and have not works?" (2:14).

Day 329

Details, Please (Part 2)

James encourages Christians, in everyday life, to view trials as opportunities for spiritual growth, to control their tongues, to make peace, to avoid favoritism, and to help the needy. The bottom line? "Therefore to him that knoweth to do good, and doeth it not, to him it is sin" (4:17).

Day 330

Quotable

- Draw nigh to God, and he will draw nigh to you. (4:8)
- The effectual fervent prayer of a righteous man availeth much. (5:16)

Day 331

UNIQUE AND UNUSUAL

For those who think it's enough just to believe in God, James says, "The devils also believe, and tremble" (2:19). Life-changing faith in Jesus is the key.

Day 332

1 PETER

AUTHORS/DATE

The apostle Peter (1:1), with the assistance of Silvanus (Silas, 5:12). Approximately AD 65.

IN TEN WORDS OR LESS

Suffering for the sake of Jesus is noble and good.

Day 333

Details, Please (Part 1)

As the early church grows, the Roman Empire begins persecuting Christians—and Peter assures them that God is still in control: "Beloved, think it not strange concerning the fiery trial which is to try you, as though some strange thing happened unto you" (4:12).

Day 334

Details, Please (Part 2)

When believers ask about the trials they face, "What is the proper response to suffering and persecution," Peter has the answer: "Rejoice, inasmuch as ye are partakers of Christ's sufferings; that, when his glory shall be revealed, ye may be glad also with exceeding joy" (4:13).

Day 335

Quotable

- Be sober, be vigilant; because your adversary the devil, as a roaring lion, walketh about, seeking whom he may devour. (5:8)

Day 336

Unique and Unusual

Peter clarifies exactly how many people rode out the great flood on Noah's ark: eight (3:20). Genesis indicates that "Noah. . .and his sons, and his wife, and his sons' wives" (Genesis 7:7) were in the boat but leaves unsaid whether any sons might have had multiple wives.

Day 337

2 PETER

AUTHOR/DATE

The apostle Peter (1:1). Probably the late 60s AD, shortly before Peter's execution.

IN TEN WORDS OR LESS

Beware of false teachers within the church.

Day 338

DETAILS, PLEASE

The Christian qualities of faith, virtue, knowledge, self-control, patience, godliness, and love (1:5–8), coupled with a reliance on scripture (1:19–21), will help believers avoid the false teachings of those who "privily shall bring in damnable heresies, even denying the Lord that bought them" (2:1).

Day 339

Quotable

- We have not followed cunningly devised fables, when we made known unto you the power and coming of our Lord Jesus Christ, but were eye-witnesses of his majesty. (1:16)

- The Lord is not slack concerning his promise, as some men count slackness; but is longsuffering to us-ward, not willing that any should perish, but that all should come to repentance. (3:9)

Day 340

Unique and Unusual

Peter wrote this letter knowing his death was near: "Shortly I must put off this my tabernacle, even as our Lord Jesus Christ hath shewed me" (1:14).

Day 341

1 JOHN

Author/Date

Not stated but according to church tradition, the apostle John. Approximately AD 92.

In Ten Words or Less

Jesus was real man just as He is real God.

Day 342

Details, Please (Part 1)

First John tackles a strange heresy that claimed Jesus had been on earth only in spirit, not in body: "Every spirit that confesseth not that Jesus Christ is come in the flesh is not of God: and this is that spirit of antichrist" (4:3).

Day 343

Details, Please (Part 2)

John wrote that he knew Jesus personally, as one "which we have looked upon, and our hands have handled" (1:1), and that knowledge leads to a saving belief in Jesus. Saving belief leads to obedience, but even when we sin, we know that God "is faithful and just to forgive us our sins" when we confess (1:9).

Day 344

Quotable

- Beloved, let us love one another: for love is of God. . . . God is love. (4:7–8)

Day 345

UNIQUE AND UNUSUAL

First John includes none of the usual features of a Bible letter—greetings, identification of the author, and the like. But it's a very warm, compassionate letter nonetheless.

Day 346

2 JOHN

AUTHOR/DATE

The apostle John according to church tradition. The author is identified only as "the elder" (1). Approximately AD 92.

IN TEN WORDS OR LESS

Beware false teachers who deny Jesus' physical life on earth.

Day 347

DETAILS, PLEASE (PART 1)

Addressed to "the elect lady and her children" (1), perhaps an actual family or, figuratively, a church, 2 John tackles the heretical idea that Jesus had not been physically present on earth, but was a spirit only.

Day 348

DETAILS, PLEASE (PART 2)

The letter may be a reaction to the "gnostics," who taught that Jesus was spirit only and that He just appeared to suffer and die on the cross. This teaching, of "a deceiver and an antichrist" (7), should be avoided at all costs—to the point of barring one's door against those who believe it (10).

Day 349

Quotable

- I beseech thee, lady, not as though I wrote a new commandment unto thee, but that which we had from the beginning, that we love one another. (5)
- This is love, that we walk after his commandments. (6)

Day 350

Unique and Unusual

Second John, one of the New Testament's four single-chapter books, is the shortest by verse count: thirteen.

Day 351

3 JOHN

AUTHOR/DATE

The apostle John according to church tradition.
The author is identified only as "the elder" (1).
Approximately AD 92.

IN TEN WORDS OR LESS

Church leaders must be humble, not proud.

Day 352

DETAILS, PLEASE

Addressed to a believer named Gaius, 3 John praises those (like Gaius and another Christian named Demetrius) who lead in "charity before the church" (6). But 3 John also has harsh words for Christians like Diotrephes, "who loveth to have the preeminence" (9) and refuse to show kindness and hospitality to traveling evangelists.

Day 353

Quotable

- I have no greater joy than to hear that my children walk in truth. (4)
- He that doeth good is of God: but he that doeth evil hath not seen God. (11)

Day 354

Unique and Unusual

Third John, one of four single-chapter books in the New Testament, is the second shortest by verse count: fourteen.

Day 355
JUDE

Author/Date

Jude (1), possibly Jesus' half brother (see Matthew 13:55; Mark 6:3). Approximately AD 82.

In Ten Words or Less

Beware of heretical teachers and their dangerous doctrines.

Day 356

Details, Please

Jude tackles the same problems Peter did in his second letter: false teachers who were leading the early church astray. "Murmurers" and "complainers" who were "walking after their own lusts" (16) were apparently using the grace of God as a cover for their sinful lifestyles—and encouraging Christian believers to do the same. True believers, Jude says, reflect God's love, show compassion, and work to pull sinners "out of the fire" (23).

Day 357

Quotable

- Ye should earnestly contend for the faith which was once delivered unto the saints. (3)
- Keep yourselves in the love of God, looking for the mercy of our Lord Jesus Christ unto eternal life. (21)

Day 358

Unique and Unusual

Jude provides details of two Old Testament events not recorded in the Old Testament: the archangel Michael's fight with Satan over the body of Moses (9) and Enoch's prophecy of God's judgment (14–15).

Day 359

REVELATION

Author/Date

John (1:1), probably the apostle. Approximately AD 95.

In Ten Words or Less

God will judge evil and reward His saints.

Day 360

Details, Please (Part 1)

Jesus Christ Himself arranges for John to receive a "revelation" of "things which must shortly come to pass" (1:1). First, in chapters 2–3, Jesus gives John words of challenge and/or encouragement for seven churches—the good, the bad, and the in-between.

Day 361

DETAILS, PLEASE (PART 2)

Then the vision turns to the actual throne room of God, where a Lamb, looking "as it had been slain" (5:6), breaks seven seals from a scroll, unleashing war, famine, and other disasters on the earth. A dragon and two beasts, allied against God, arise to demand the worship of earth's people who have not been killed in the earlier catastrophes.

Day 362

DETAILS, PLEASE (PART 3)

The satanic forces and the people who follow them incur seven "vials of the wrath of God" (16:1), which bring plagues, darkness, and huge hailstones on earth. The upheaval destroys "Babylon the great" (18:2), the evil and arrogant world system, just before an angel from heaven seizes Satan, "that old serpent" (20:2), and imprisons him for one thousand years.

Day 363

Details, Please (Part 4)

After a brief release to instigate a worldwide war, Satan is thrown into "the lake of fire and brimstone," where he will be "tormented day and night for ever and ever" (20:10). God unveils "a new heaven and a new earth" (21:1), where He will "wipe away all tears" (21:4) from His people's eyes.

Day 364

Quotable

- Blessed is he that readeth, and they that hear the words of this prophecy, and keep those things which are written therein. (1:3)
- Worthy is the Lamb that was slain to receive power, and riches, and wisdom, and strength, and honour, and glory, and blessing. (5:12)

Day 365

Unique and Unusual

Revelation is an example of "apocalyptic literature," the only such book in the New Testament. *Apocalyptic* implies "revealing secret information." The book of Revelation identifies Jesus Christ as the "Alpha and Omega" (1:8) and reveals the number 666 as a sign of "the beast" (13:18).

THE MOST IMPORTANT QUESTION
ANYONE COULD ASK...

Who is Jesus?

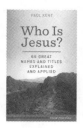

For each of 66 names and attributes of Jesus, *Who Is Jesus?* gives you a ten-word summary, a longer description, a listing of key verses, a practical application, and more. Patterned after the 2 million-copy bestseller *Know Your Bible*—and written by the same author, Paul Kent—*Who Is Jesus?* promises insight for believers and seekers of any age or background. Small and easy-to-read, it's packed with helpful information on Jesus—the Alpha and Omega, Creator, Good Shepherd, and Word Made Flesh, plus 62 other fascinating descriptions. You'll get to know Jesus better. . .and deepen your relationship with the most important Person of all time!

Paperback / 978-1-64352-247-0 / $2.99

Find This and More from Barbour
Books at Your Favorite Bookstore
www.barbourbooks.com